# 40 Common Errors IN RACQUETBALL and How to Correct Them

# 40 Common Errors IN RACQUETBALL and How to Correct Them

Arthur Shay and Terry Fancher

cbi Contemporary Books, Inc.
Chicago

**Library of Congress Cataloging in Publication Data**

Shay, Arthur.
40 common errors in racquetball and how to correct them.

Includes index.
1. Racquetball. I. Fancher, Terry, joint author.
II. Title.
GV1017.R3S48 1978 796.34'3 77-23707
ISBN 0-8092-7704-2
ISBN 0-8092-7703-4 pbk.


Published by Contemporary Books, Inc.
180 North Michigan Avenue, Chicago, Illinois 60601
Manufactured in the United States of America
Library of Congress Catalog Card Number: 77-23707
International Standard Book Number: 0-8092-7704-2 (cloth)
0-8092-7703-4 (paper)

Published simultaneously in Canada by
Beaverbooks
953 Dillingham Road
Pickering, Ontario L1W 1Z7
Canada

## Dedication

This book is dedicated to all of the smiling faces at Community Builders, Incorporated, home of the United States Racquetball Association and National Racquetball Club, and to my parents.

I would like to thank the following people for their assistance in compiling this book: Bob Kendler, Evie Kendler, John Lynch, Dottie Trauscht, Lee Duda, National Racquetball Magazine, Leach Industries, Marty Hogan, Jean Sauser, and my bride, Kip Kendler Fancher.

Special thanks to the Court Club Circuit, Skokie, Illinois, and Sky Harbor, Northbrook, Illinois, for the use of their courts.

Terry Fancher,
National Executive Coordinator
U.S. Racquetball Association
Skokie, Illinois

# Contents

# Introduction

Socrates believed that the best possible teaching situation was a log with a teacher at one end and a student at the other.

Education hasn't changed very much since 399 BC. when Socrates died, in part for his teaching method.

As author-photographer of or collaborator on some 40 sports and educational books, I am not really prepared to die for my methods of instruction. My personal background (before I became the official photographer for the U.S. Racquetball Association) was as a *Life* reporter and photographer. It was on *Life* that I learned the value of simplicity in the sharing of information. One big picture tells the story better than a whole series of small step-by-step pictures. Clarity was held in high regard.

Judging from the letters I've received from readers of my books, less *is* really more, and writers had better stick to the facts.

Having now spent five years playing Low A Class Racquetball for fun and shooting pictures of racquetball for *National Racquetball Magazine,* the *New York Times, Time, Sports Illustrated, Horizon, TWA Ambassador,* and many more, I have come to feel that we racquetballers are the fastest growing misunderstood minority in the country.

With a rate of growth exceeding that of tennis as I write, racquetball is still only at the beginning of its adolescence—and, like any adolescent, largely and annoyingly misunderstood. I tried to suggest a story on racquetball to an old friend, an editor of *Sports Illustrated.* He said, "Racquetball? Is that the one they play with the wooden racquet or the sawed-off tennis racquet?" (A year later Sports Illustrated Enterprises announced a vast franchise deal for 100 racquetball clubs all over the world!)

A Chicago newspaper breathlessly announced a boom in squash because nine—

count 'em, *nine* new squash clubs opened in New York! Why, I get requests for racquetball pictures from nine publications a *week!* And within thirty miles of where I live near Chicago there are some seventy new court clubs—not counting the terrific facilities at Northwest Suburban Y, the famous "Glass Court Y," with its controversial glass front wall designed by U. S. R. A.'s handball-playing czar, Bob Kendler.

Racquetball has its Babe Ruth—aging Charlie Brumfield, creaking into TV coverage of racquetball at the advanced age of twenty-eight. At 19, Marty Hogan has earned or won $100,000 in racquetball already—and the prize money is growing as large corporations buy up the small racquetball equipment companies. A record entry list of junior players swamped U. S. R. A. Commissioner Chuck Leve and tournament arranger Joe Ardito. "At each junior tournament I feel those 15-year-olds breathing on my neck," says Marty Hogan, who has won 15 of his last 18 tournaments.

"There'll be sixteen-year-old pros!" Ardito exclaimed, only half joking because Hogan, having earned nearly $100,000 in the past year playing racquetball and plugging its products, was standing nearby. How does it feel to be a World Class champion at nineteen and threatened by a youth movement? Come to think of it, I saw it happen at the Olympics, when Romania's Nadia Comaneci, at thirteen, swept everything in sight.

But the real racquetball story is in clubs, such as the Court House chain in Chicago, where families have taken up the sport as a group exercise and pleasure program. It's airline stewardesses playing each other in leagues that have begun to expand from San Diego and Chicago to the rest of the country. Racquetball has even been taken up by the formerly nonathletic head of this publishing company and by the extremely athletic woman who edits these words.

Slowly, New York—three courts so far—and New Jersey—about 15—and Delaware and Cincinnati and Atlanta are building clubs. The fun, the frustration, the wonderful feeling that an hour of racquetball and a shower adds to one's day will become much more common. So much the better. Travelers will be able to play more away from home. The equipment companies will be able to offer the pros, especially women, more prize money.

To celebrate the completion of this book, my collaborator, Terry Fancher, rated among the top sixteen players in the country, challenged me to a game of singles. It was hard work—for me—but I (the reigning *handball* champ of the Sky Harbor Club) scored twelve points on the kid.

"You've been reading the book," Fancher said, obviously pleased by my progress.

So use this book to correct *your* mistakes, too. But, most importantly, have fun playing racquetball!

Arthur Shay

# Chapter 1
# Grips

# MISTAKE

## Slipped grip

Many of the bad shots in racquetball can be traced to the grip. The most common error in this area is letting the hand slip gradually to the right as shown. Hitting the ball with the racquet in this position results in a tightening of the wrist action necessary for a good stroke. The ball, struck when the hand is in this poor position, will often hit on the floor, short of the wall, or take an otherwise unintended path.

# CORRECTION

Looking down at your grip, your thumb and forefinger should make a V along the handle when the racquet face is in the up and down (perpendicular to the floor) position.

Hitting the ball with the wrist in this position permits the wrist to rotate freely and impart a degree of "snap" to the ball as you hit it.

If your grip error is compounded by a sudden relaxation of the fingers at the moment you strike the ball, try squeezing the racquet hard just before and during the moment of impact.

This will help keep your grip from slipping or loosening.

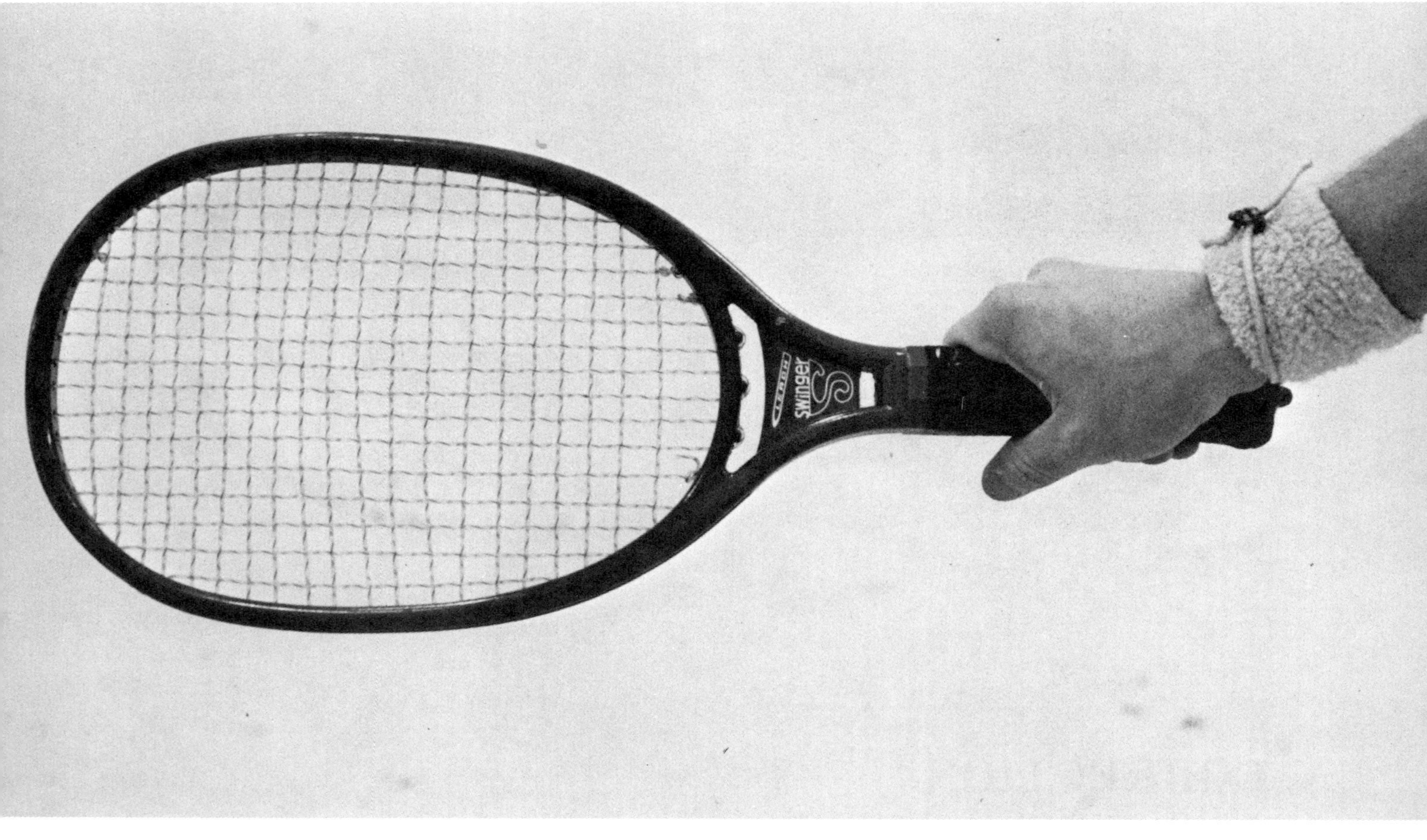


# MISTAKE

## Turning grip

When the hand is positioned too far to the left on the racquet handle or, as is more often the case, gradually slips too far to the left, the ball will be undercut and carry too high on the front wall.

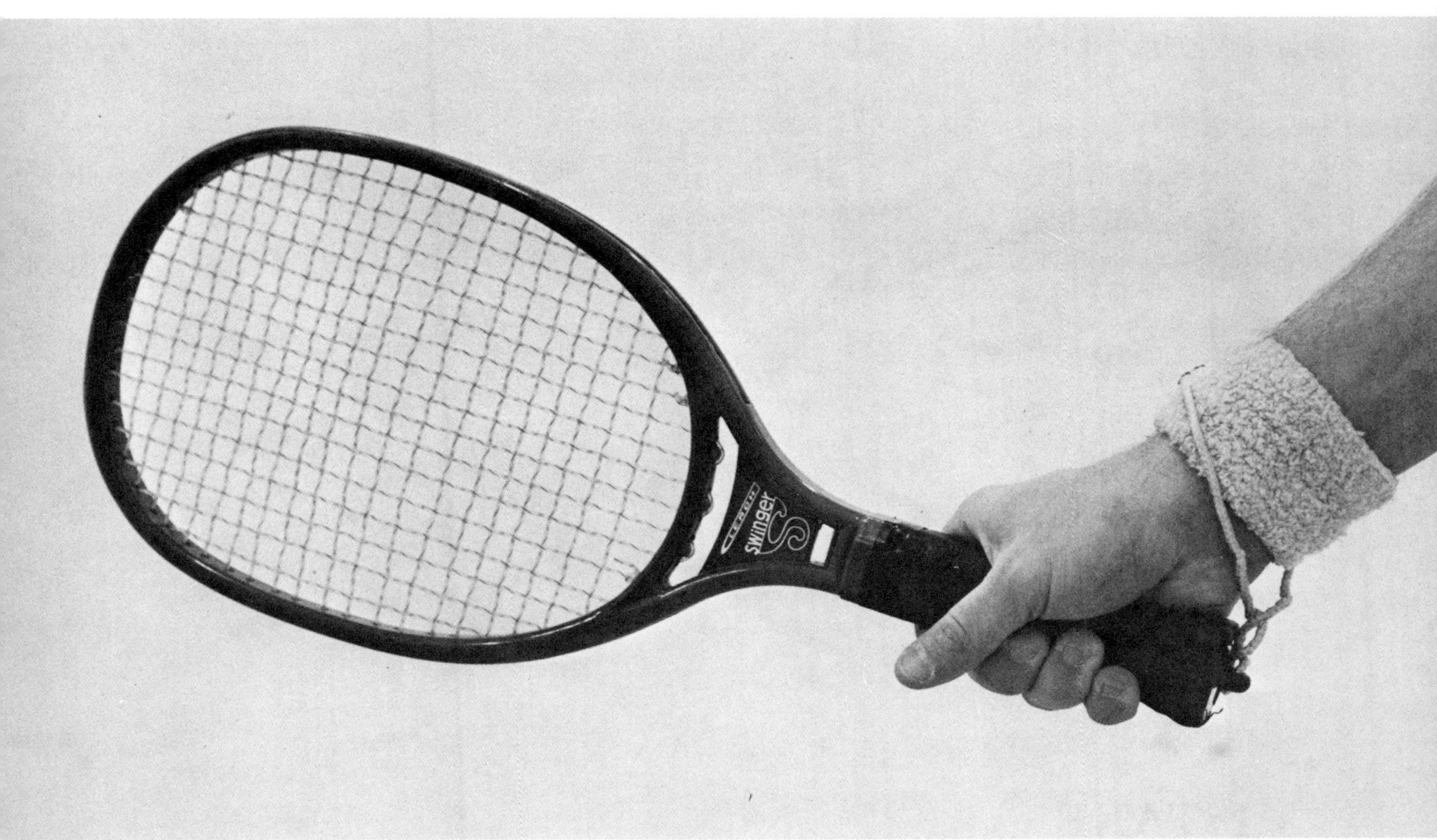


## CORRECTION

Move your gripping hand so that the V of the gripping thumb and forefinger is at the top of the handle shaft, looking down at it. A determined squeeze just before, during, and after hitting the ball will help insure the accuracy of your shot.

Periodically during play, relax your grip on the handle and then resume it. This helps your grip from freezing into a wrong position or gradually slipping into one.

If you do have a problem of slippage, try using a lightweight glove without fingertips. This offers a little more traction without dulling the important racquet "feel" of the lower three fingers.

# MISTAKE

## Thumbs up

Many players permit their thumb to rest along the shaft of the racquet, and some players who do this develop fairly good hitting techniques by making unorthodox compensations for this mistake.

The thumb is the strongest single element in the grip, and if not used properly, the racquet will wobble at the moment of impact, resulting in inaccurate placement of the ball.

## CORRECTION

Firmly wrap your thumb around the racquet shaft (watch that V) until that thumb touches your first or second finger. Keeping this slight contact between thumb and fingers will automatically tighten your grip. Adding a slight squeeze at the moment of impact will help some players who have developed a "wobble," as it helps in the other grip errors.

Ideally, the racquet at the moment of impact should be at a right angle to the floor—straight up and down.

Your "grip practice" sessions should include straightening your racquet into this position as you hit a series of balls.

# MISTAKE

## Backhand grip faults

Backhand mistakes are more common than forehand mistakes because many beginning (and advanced!) players find it difficult to move the gripping hand the necessary quarter- to half-inch on the shaft to compensate for the difference between the backhand and forehand strokes.

If you use the forehand grip for a backhand shot, you will tend to rotate the head of the racquet upward, causing the ball to hit too high on the front wall or, in any case, not precisely where you wanted to place it.

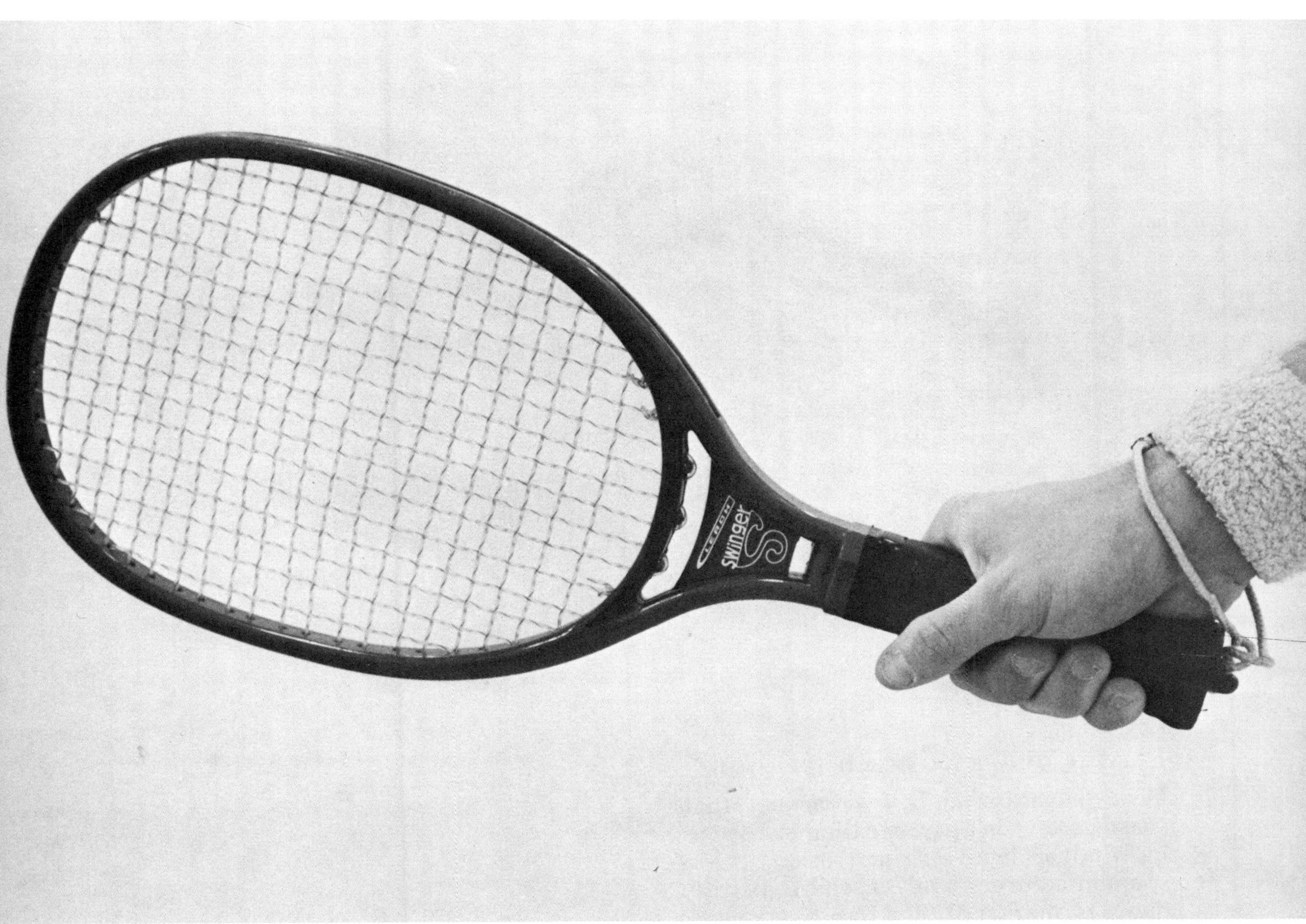


## CORRECTION

The idea of slightly shifting the grip is to keep the face of the racquet perpendicular to the floor as you hit the ball. Moving your hand an eighth- to quarter-inch in a slight clockwise motion as you're getting ready to hit a backhand shot will keep your racquet perpendicular to the floor as you hit and give you the accuracy you want.

In effect, you are moving the face of the racquet slightly to make up for the difference in wrist position between forehand and backhand stroke.

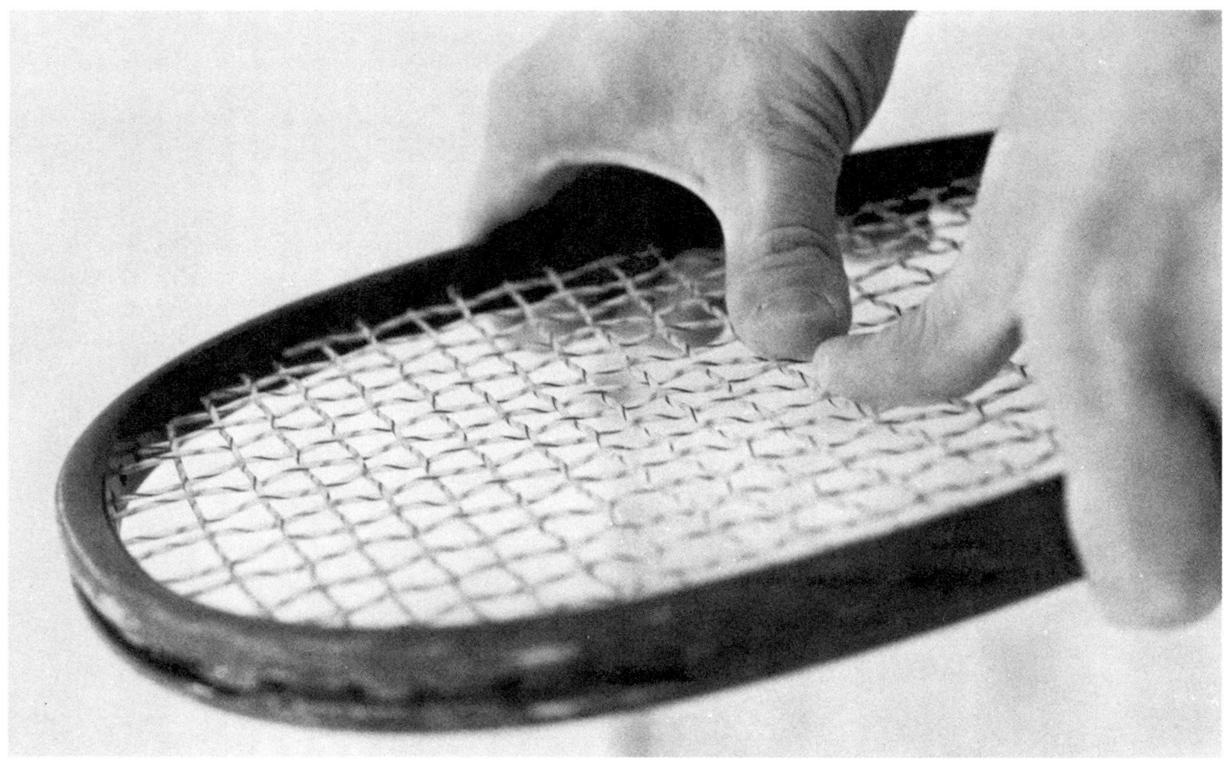

# MISTAKE

## Playing under too much "pressure"

Most players who buy a racquet that "feels good" don't pay attention to a seemingly minor detail—string tension.

Manufacturers tend to send their racquets to market rather tightly strung—between 28 and 35 pounds of pressure.

Playing with a racquet that "tight" gives you a good twanging sound but also is often costing you points. That is because a ball will leave a tightly strung racquet just a little too quickly, and a certain loss of shot control results.

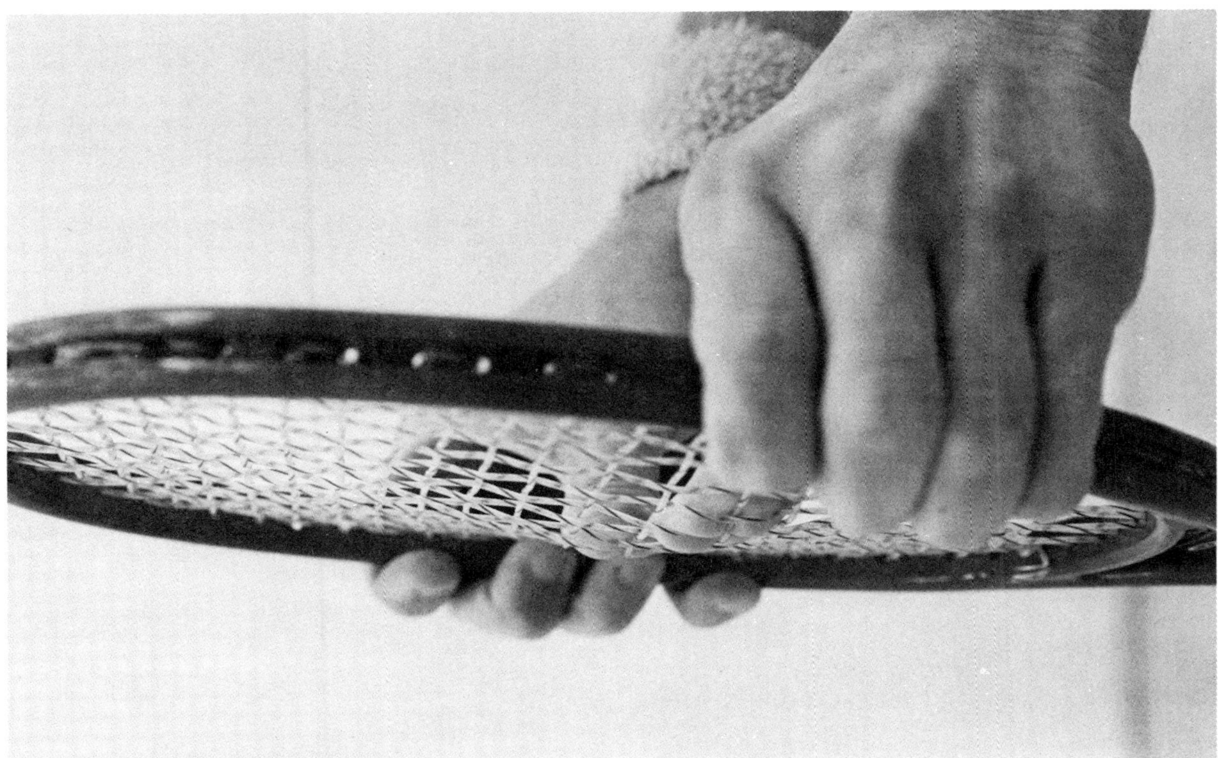

## CORRECTION

Have your club pro restring your racquet at a lower tension—18 to 25 pounds is ideal.

This will permit the ball to remain on the strings a split second longer—just long enough to give the good or improving player a little more control than is attainable with the "tight" racquet.

Racquetball (and tennis and squash) pros often refer to the "sweet spot" on their racquets, the area (when the racquet is strung properly for tension) that imparts the maximum speed and control to their shot.

There is controversy over whether fiber or metal racquets have a better "sweet spot." This must be determined by trial on the court.

Meanwhile, check the tension of your strings. They're probably tighter than you think!

## Chapter 2

# Body positions

# MISTAKE

## Improper warm-up

It is not advisable to enter the racquetball court and immediately start to play, hoping to warm up as the game progresses. Muscles are temperamental wonders and are given to stiffening up and causing pain in other ways if they are not gradually stretched into readiness.

You may get the ball to the wall, but the body and mind tend to stay behind without a good warm-up.

It is also inadvisable to begin a game directly after five minutes of stretching and knee bends without warming up your racquetball skills.

# CORRECTION

Many pros like to do dynamic tension exercises, pushing as hard as they can against the wall. Knee bends and stretches are good warm-up procedures, as is jogging in place. Sit-ups are common. Marty Hogan likes to run around the court before he begins the serious business of practicing shots before a match. National champ Davey Bledsoe likes to sit on an invisible chair, supporting himself by his back muscle and the long muscles of his thighs.

Pro Jay Jones, a movie stunt man, likes to climb six or eight flights of stairs to warm up for a match!

A series of forehands, backhands, and a few shots off the back wall and side walls should complete your warm-up before a match.

# MISTAKE

## Unbending body position

Too many racquetball players are unbending in their approach to the game. It is a mistake to play from a position that's too erect. Flexibility is the key to the game, and making shots from too high a body position, with legs too close together, wastes a good part of the body's power base.

When hit from a "too high" body position, the ball tends to float to the front wall too high, providing an easy mark for a strong foe.

Adding to the difficulties of this bad stance, the racquet head tends to tilt down in compensation for the body's poor position, and control of the ball is seriously hampered.

# CORRECTION

Your feet should be separated and the stance "closed"—achieving a lower, more comfortable base of power. This will allow the body to rotate more freely and, by extension, permit the racquet to transfer the body's power to the ball, giving you harder, faster shots.

It is easier to keep the racquet perpendicular to the floor from a good body position, and this will result in more accuracy. Even more desirable, you will be able to keep the ball low on the wall and much harder to return.

# MISTAKE

## Bad backhand body position

Many players do not pay enough attention to the position of their bodies during backhand strokes. They forget that racquetball is a "sideways" game, played largely (ideally, that is) with the body facing one side wall or the other. Swinging head-on, facing the front wall, they do not make enough use of their bodies, and their games rarely improve. When they do make heroic retrieves, the ball just barely makes it to the wall.

# CORRECTION

Your wrist should be cocked and the racquet held well back. Your stance is balanced and *facing the side wall.* Your hips and shoulders now can be rotated easily in order to get wrist and racquet into position for hitting the ball with the body's entire force—not just the wrist's!

As in other sports involving the transfer of the body's power to a ball (tennis, baseball, golf), the "moment of truth"— of a "good hit"—can actually be felt. It is a feeling the racquetball player should work toward in practice.

It is not uncommon for a pro to try 200 shots from this backhand position, aiming at specific "invisible" spots on the wall. To carry this type of practice one step further, Jay Jones and Charlie Brumfield have been experimenting with putting patches of tape on the walls at crucial aiming points.

# MISTAKE

## Wall crashing

Racing toward either side wall, it is easy to overrun the ball and crash into the wall, usually shoulder high with the arm pinioned between body and wall.

# CORRECTION

To avoid overrunning that results in wall crashing, practice hitting from racquet and arm's length from the wall. Do a series of ten shots forehand and backhand from each wall, trying to hit "wallpaper" balls—balls very close to the wall.

Even in a frantic rush to the ball, you shouldn't have to come closer than 3 feet or so—theoretically.

OK, a crash is imminent. Learn to break your crash by using the hand and arm nearest the wall as a kind of shock absorber, a spring that lets the body hit the wall with some insulation from the direct shock.

As swimmers and veteran handball players do, then learn to use that braking (not breaking) arm to push off and get back into a good defensive position, instead of crumbling on the spot.

# MISTAKE

## Nonsupport by body

Racquetball is such an "easy" sport to play that the "easiness" interferes with progress for many players.

By far the most common racquetball error is poor body stance, particularly positioning the body to face the front wall for backhand and then compounding the error in their forehand.

This error usually goes with a poor base of support (the body) and generally involves hitting the ball while the body is too high.

Loss of power and accuracy result, as well as that other hallmark of the unimproving player—balls hit far too high and ineffectively to the front wall.

# CORRECTION

The secret of racquetball is getting your body to face the side wall as you swing. Get those toes pointed to the right wall for your forehand shots and to the left wall for those backhands. (Vice versa for lefties.)

The body should be low and springy—ready to go in any direction instantly.

You now will be able to step into the ball, rotating your shoulders and waist and transmitting your body's power to the ball. You also will be able to move easily to your next shot rather than waddle flat-footedly.

# MISTAKE

## Not using your head

You have just hit the ball to your opponent who is behind you. For some reason, you neglect to turn your head to see what he is going to do. Wham! He puts the ball past you on one side or the other.

# CORRECTION

There are two objects your eye must follow constantly in racquetball: the ball and your opponent.

It's not necessary to lock your gaze on either 100 percent of the time, an impossibility anyway. After you hit the ball, your head should move in quick, neck-turning motions to observe the ball on its way to your opponent. You shouldn't change your body position "just to have a look", but incorporate a kind of neck-swiveling motion into your game, a series of split-second "snapshots" that take an overall picture of opponent and ball relative to your own momentary position.

As you learn to do this, your awareness will increase by leaps and bounds. You will be able to anticipate where to run for your next shot just from studying your opponent's stance and general "set up" for his shot.

Keep that head moving!

# MISTAKE

## Backing up

The ball comes off the front wall at medium speed. The player backs up, finally makes some sort of return—and finds himself off balance for a soft shot up front. Backing up literally keeps your back to the wall and may get you in trouble.

## CORRECTION

Backing up should be done by running in the direction the ball is retreating or, if necessary, in a kind of sideways, crab-like series of steps.

It is easier to stop your backward motion this way, and your body has a better platform from which to operate when you move forward. By quick glances and turns of the neck, it is possible to keep an eye on your opponent during this maneuver. Your return shot then can be played to his or her weakness or poor position. You also will be facing a side wall, already in fair shape for your next shot.

# Chapter 3
# Serves

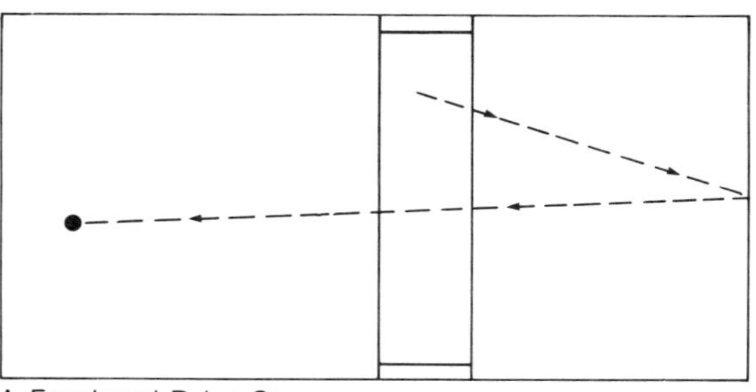

A Forehand Drive Serve

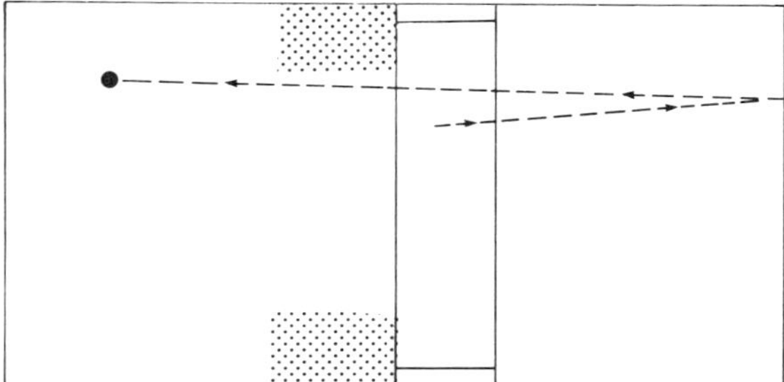

B Drive Serve (to left) Missing Crack Zone

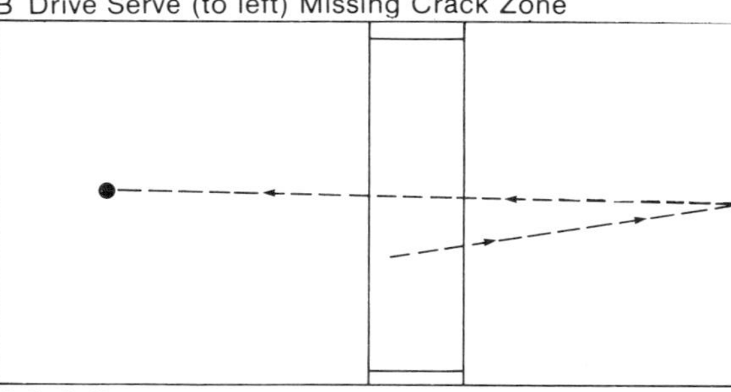

C Lob Serve

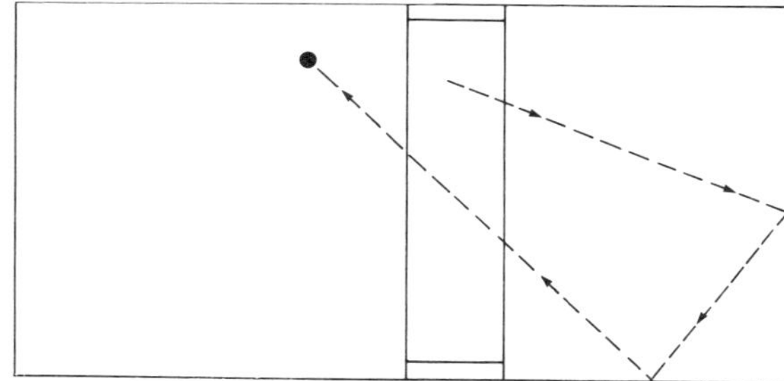

D Z Serve

# MISTAKE

## Service faults

There are three basic kinds of serves in racquetball, each with its own built-in possibilities for error.

The Lob Serve starts with the server in the box a little left of center. Ideally, the ball is hit gently so that it arcs back toward the left rear wall, coming down about six feet from the back wall. In practice, however, the ball often is hit right up the middle. This offers your opponent a big, fat, lazy ball to kill or otherwise give you a hard time.

The Drive Serve is delivered low and hard from the center of the serving box, just passes the short line, and hits the wall within five feet of the line. In actual play this shot is often blown, and it comes off the wall in perfect position for a forehand or backhand kill by your opponent.

The Z Serve is the most difficult for the new racquetball player. The shot starts from a little left of center in the serving box, hits the front wall near the right corner, caroms to the sidewall, then travels all the way back to the left wall just short of the deep corner. It then, ideally, "dies" irretrievably. (Oh, how beautiful it is to watch one's opponent flail at a perfect Z Serve!)

The cardinal mistake is to hit the side wall first—an instant out. Beyond that, most bad Zs are hit too far from the front corner and then describe either imperfect Zs or, worse, other letters. These often spell "out" because they tend to offer opponents a set-up.

In all serves, hitting to your opponent's strength gives him or her an unnecessary advantage.

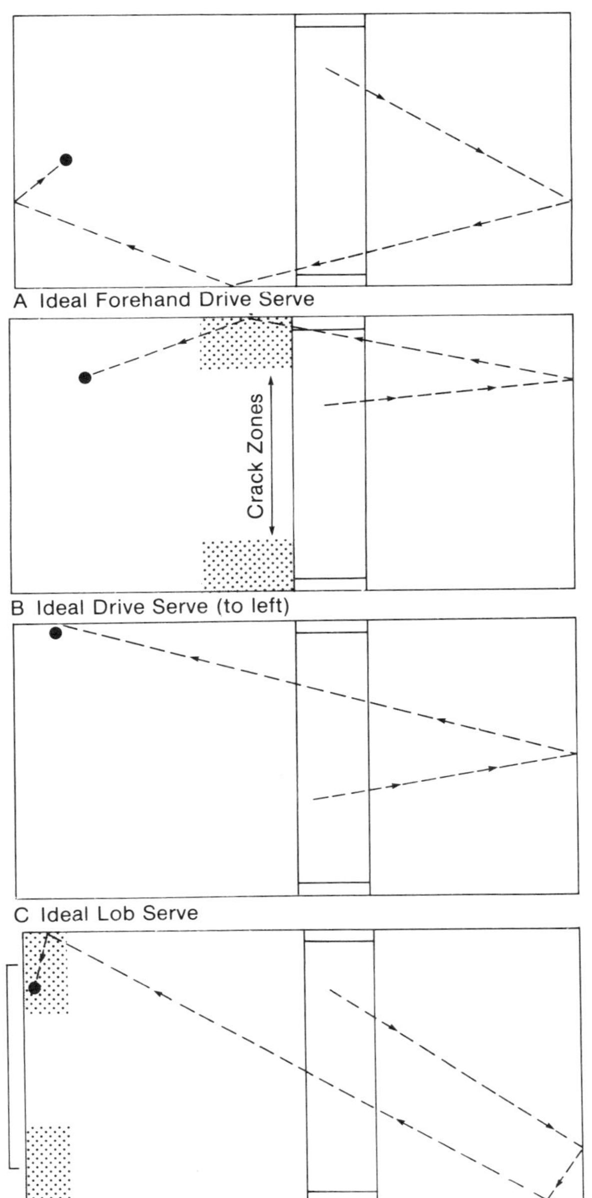

A Ideal Forehand Drive Serve

B Ideal Drive Serve (to left)

C Ideal Lob Serve

D Ideal Z Serve

# CORRECTION

Avoid the middle of the court when serving; start thinking "corner, corner, corner." Keep your opponent off balance by serving into the deep corners and alternating your serves to these corners.

Serving deeply will give you time to get into the center-court defensive position (an imaginary six-foot circle just behind the short line).

Veteran pro and teacher Jean Sauser says, "Serving gives you your first chance to outsmart your opponent. Take advantage of it."

Practice the Lob until you can make it land where you want it to land—about six feet from the back wall along one side or the other.

Don't be afraid to use your power on a Drive Serve. Sometimes speed will stand in for accuracy and get you a winner.

The Z Serve should be practiced more than the Drive and Lob together because, when mastered, it can improve your game measurably. Pick out an aiming area on the front wall and keep hitting to it. A Z Serve is sort of a billiard shot; it will reward you handsomely when you incorporate it into your game. It's the one shot that the good B player must learn before ascending to the As.

It sometimes helps to put little tape marks on the wall as aiming points, the way pros Jay Jones and Charlie Brumfield have done experimentally.

# MISTAKE

## Not studying opponent

Serving without properly maintaining a continuous study of your opponent often results in the loss of your serve by a fast pass shot on either side. You had the initiative, starting play, and ended up with the feeling that you weren't quite "ready."

## CORRECTION

There is a degree of instant "psyching" going on between server and receiver just before the serve. There is a shuffling of feet, a focus of attention by the receiver, a sway perhaps, as many tennis players do to keep their concentration and to keep from freezing up and losing alertness.

Just before serving you should glance at the receiver. This informs him that you know exactly where he is, and he won't be able to surprise you by darting in to hit a serve on the fly or otherwise outmaneuver you.

By studying your opponent just before you serve, you can become an expert at detecting whether he or she is leaning to one side or the other or playing farther to one side than the other. Take instant advantage of this intelligence and serve to the weakness!

# MISTAKE

## Jammed serve

A jammed serve results from hitting the ball when it's too close to your body. Your elbow is crushed into your body, and the shot is weak and generally ineffective. The server who jams himself in this way invariably pops the ball up too high, leaving an easy hanger for a competent foe.

## CORRECTION

When serving, the ball should be dropped away from and in front of the body, allowing enough room for a full swing. The timing of the hard serve should be worked on so that when the ball is struck, it is below knee level and travels a low, hard path to the wall, snapping back as a tough shot for your opponent to return.

Practice dropping the ball so that you can hit it with optimum power from the best position. Soon you will be able to move the ball all over your opponent's territory from the same serving position, adding a tool to your arsenal.

Remember: the key is to drop the ball far enough away from your body and hit it while it is below knee level.

# Chapter 4
# Strokes

# MISTAKE

### Danger of early stroke

Attempting to stroke the ball before it's in proper position to be hit results in scatter-shooting, loss of power, and blown points and games.

Shooting too soon is a common error even among physically fit and fast players. Often, they get to the ball too soon and swing while the ball is still momentarily hovering "off" the rear foot. Much power and accuracy is lost this way.

Early stroking results in shots that drive otherwise well-coordinated players to pound the wall with their racquets without comprehending what went wrong.

## CORRECTION

The tendency to shoot too soon can be corrected by a degree of mind control: mind that you don't swing until the ball passes the center line of your body.

What's involved is a kind of "instant waiting," holding off until your shoulders, waist, and wrist can pour power into the stroke. The shot then will have considerably more speed than when hit too soon. Also, the ball will hit the front wall much lower, giving your opponent a difficult shot to return rather than a hanger that he or she can kill.

This vital timing sequence can be practiced, forehand and backhand, by throwing the ball, waist high, against the rear wall or one of the side walls. Practice waiting, waiting, waiting until your body moves into proper hitting position, that is, so the moment of impact occurs when the ball is just past the body's midpoint, en route over the front (lead) foot.

Advanced player should be aware that the immortal Charlie Brumfield, studying Art Shay sequence pictures of Marty Hogan, thinks that "power" racquetball requires hitting the ball off the *rear* foot. Give it a try.

# MISTAKE

## Stiff-wrist shooting

The wrist often is overlooked as a source of errors in racquetball. It is often the culprit in a bad shot. When the wrist is kept too rigid during the stroke, the ball is pushed rather than stroked to the front wall. Much loss of power results from stiff-wrist shooting.

## CORRECTION

Think of your wrist as your personal cobra, ready to strike. It should be held cocked well back at the start of a stroke and at the moment of contact "snapped" or "rolled over." You're after that feeling of sudden achievement and power you get after making a good shot or good connection with the ball. It's a surge of coordinated power that starts at the shoulders, courses through the waist, and flows to the ball via that cobra wrist.

Whether you think of it as a cobra, a sudden "snap," or an uncocking of a lethal weapon, the idea is to keep hitting in practice until you get that perfect feeling, that perfect placement, that sense of imparting a little more power and accuracy to the ball than you thought yourself capable of doing.

Then practice recapturing that wonderful feeling.

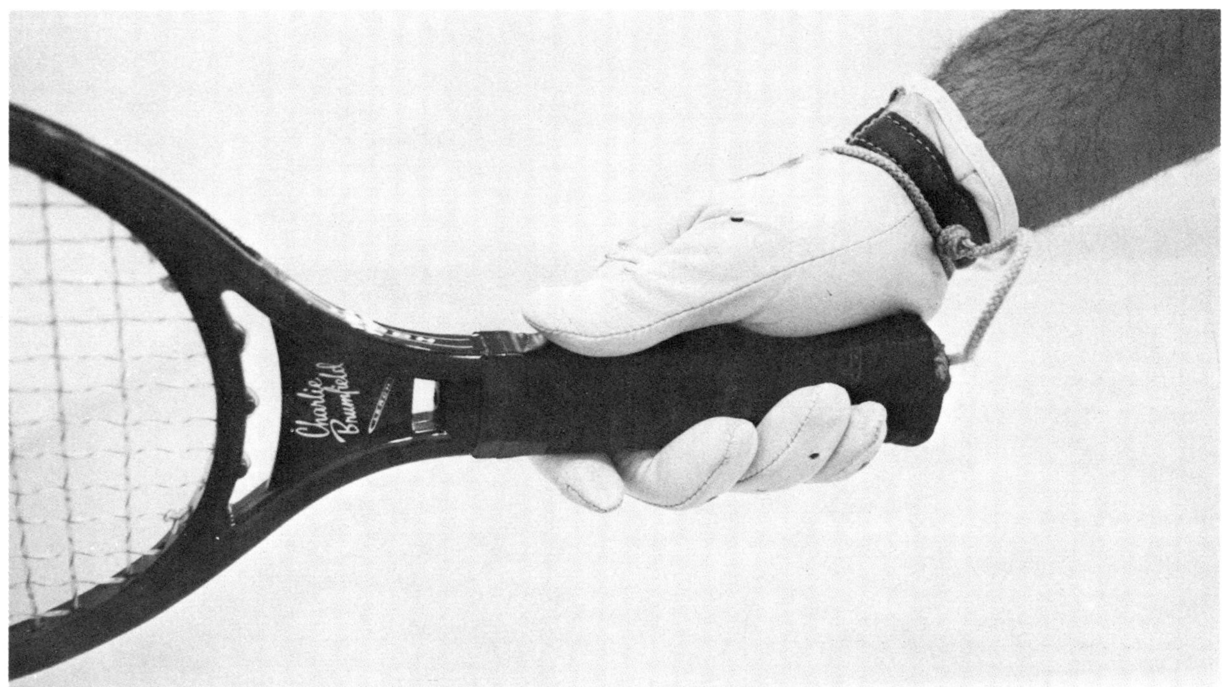


# MISTAKE

## Swatting the backhand

There is a tendency in backhand shots to swat the ball instead of stroking it.

The fault generally is compounded by the racquet's face turning upward and poor or shifting thumb position. This will loft the ball toward the ceiling and if it does not make it to the front wall, allow an easy return by your adversary.

## CORRECTION

The swat is generally caused by poor body position, by forgetting that racquetball is largely a sideways game and each shot must start way back and end up way forward, with the ball being hit at approximately the midpoint of your arc. As your swing improves, your wrist should cock and "snap," releasing its power to the ball.

The other villain in swatting is often, of all things, the *thumb!* Your thumb is the key to good backhand shots because it commands your hand's grip on the racquet, or should. The thumb should be kept well down the handle, wrapped tightly around the racquet, crowding that index finger snugly. The face of the racquet, most of the time, should be perpendicular to the floor or parallel to the front wall if that is easier for you to remember during the instant crises of the game. With the racquet correctly aligned and your thumb ruling out racquet-waggle, the ball will head for the front wall with more speed and much more control.

Don't forget the last part of your swing, the follow-through. It is the follow-through coming after a good wrist-snap that gives you that satisfying, solid sense of having powered the ball.

# MISTAKE

## Arm crimp

Shortening the arm's swing at the elbow occurs most commonly in shots off the back wall. The arm crimps against the body, and the shot has poor accuracy and practically no power. The difficulty begins with, of all things, the legs, which must move the body sufficiently away from the ball so that the arm can extend in a good swinging arc.

## CORRECTION

The arm must be held well back so that it can make a much larger arc than the errant player usually uses for this shot. The legs must move the body far enough away so that the arm doesn't have to crimp at the moment of impact. This usually involves a backward step.

A good follow-through rounds out a good stroke.

This is a good shot to incorporate into your training routine if you periodically find the ball jammed up against your body and your elbow working overtime.

# MISTAKE

## Overusing overhand

The ball comes to the floor of the deep-court hard and bounces high off the back wall. Because the ball is way up there, there is a tendency to return it using an overhand stroke.

This stroke contains a higher percentage of built-in trouble for more players than any stroke in racquetball.

# CORRECTION

A sidearm stroke—either forehand or backhand—is indicated in this situation. It offers more control of the ball, and at the finish of the stroke you are in better position for your next shot than after the overhand.

In practice you should throw balls against the back wall at various heights and go after them with confidence—sidearm.

# MISTAKE

## High-flying ball

Often, the height at which a shot is taken is the crucial factor, or the culprit in a bad shot.

If the ball is taken when it is too high, it tends to fly too high off the racquet, and most of the player's energy will be wasted trying to make a compensating body or wrist move.

## CORRECTION

Practice hitting the ball when it is close to the floor. You will have power, surprise, and accuracy working for you if you develop this rare ability.

Most pros diagnose the general inability or unwillingness of their students to "get down," "bend," or "reach" as the prime reason for not advancing in ability or moving up in class. This is especially true of relatively "good" players. They learn to retrieve well enough so that they don't have to bend very much—unless they come up against a tough opponent. By then, if they haven't practiced getting down and hitting low, it's too late.

In your warm-ups and practice sessions, hit a series of 25 low forehands and 25 backhands before playing.

# Chapter 5
# Corners

# MISTAKE

## Getting cornered

Players who do *almost* everything well at the back wall often make the mistake of "painting themselves into the corner."

They end up too close to the back wall to take an effective swing. Sometimes their racquets clatter into the wall. They tend to get angry at themselves in this situation or angry at the ball, which is already out of range.

# CORRECTION

Body awareness is the only answer to correcting this common mistake. You must know or learn how much room you have at all times relative to the walls and, especially, the corners.

Pros practice this awareness by tossing or hitting balls into the rear corners and taking them with the best possible complete stroke. In short—it's a lot easier not to paint yourself into one of the corners.

# MISTAKE

## Suicide in the front corner

The corners of the racquetball court are built-in trouble areas, especially the front ones. A common disaster area is the right front corner. A ball comes slowly off the back wall, bounces mid-court, and heads for the front wall near the right side of the court. You have plenty of time. Your opponent is cowering, waiting for your kill.

So what do you do? You powder the ball into the corner, right wall, front wall—and *your* body! You've actually hit yourself by charging in and blocking the corner.

# CORRECTION

The percentage shot here is to hit across your body to the front wall and out into the court. Hit hard if possible but soft if you've just made a long run. Aim front wall to deep-court, or aim to hit the side wall, after the front wall, as far from your opponent's position as you can manage.

The trick is not to panic because of being "cornered," and it's wise to practice getting yourself into the corners and out of them by throwing the ball into them from back-court and chasing forward to retrieve them properly—without committing racquetball hara kiri, that is, clobbering yourself to the delight of your opponent.

# Chapter 6
# Back wall play

# MISTAKE

## Back wall woes

Many players tend to regard the back wall as an enemy instead of a friend and rush to hit the ball before it can rebound off the back wall. Or, even after letting the ball hit the back wall, they lose that essential sideways stance and end up hitting the ball (if indeed they do) lightly, with the body erroneously parallel to the front and back walls. Often, they make the additional mistake of letting the ball crowd their body, resulting in an awkward swing.

# CORRECTION

A more experienced player will time the ball so that he swings his body into proper hitting position as the ball comes into range. The point is to keep the ball at a proper distance so that it doesn't crowd your shot.

The real trick is to face sideways (forehand or backhand, it's still sideways) and leave enough room for a full swing. This is often one of those racquetball situations in which there is more time to get set than you think there is.

Practice this shot by throwing or hitting balls high to the front wall and letting them come back to the rear wall. Time them so that you swing as they come out six feet from the back wall. As your skill improves, you should be able to cut this distance down to one racquet-length from the rear wall. This is a "retrieve" shot, defensive usually, and often a desperation shot, so hit it hard and aim it to come well back in the court to give your opponent the most trouble you can.

# MISTAKE

## Indecision

Racquetball is a kind of instant chess, in which the time limit on decisions runs out every few seconds.

One of the decisions that's tough to make quickly is whether to take the ball in deep-court or to let it hit the back wall and play it as it comes off. A wrong decision results in a poor shot, often an uncoordinated "push" instead of a stroke.

# CORRECTION

Each instant decision must be based on whether or not you can get a good, full swing as you hit the ball. This series of decisions may be practiced by flipping the ball behind you to the wall and hitting a series of forehand or backhand returns, whichever body position is easier for you to assume under the stress of a fast shot.

On either side, you must remember to allow room for your swing so as not to "jam" your arm as you swing.

Another good exercise is, starting at the service box, to flip the ball to the back wall in a high, slow lob. Race back and try to make the best possible decision—play it off the back wall, on the bounce, backhand, or forehand.

The more of these decisions you practice the better equipped you will be for the rigors of actual play.

# MISTAKE

## Up against the wall

The beginner and intermediate player generally don't get enough "use" from the back wall.

It can, in certain deep-court, semi-desperate situations, be a real stumbling block, leading players into contortions. Contortions often result in lost points and games.

## CORRECTION

A rear wall shot often can be timed so that the back wall is used as a substitute front wall. The ball can be slammed into, hit hard, and aimed for the front wall.

It's a good idea to stay especially alert after a back wall slam such as this because you may have given your opponent an easy set-up.

Still, in your practice regimen, or even during a short warm-up, you should hit a few balls that come off the back wall right back at that back wall as hard as you can.

# Chapter 7
# Ceiling shots

## MISTAKE

### Close-in ceiling shots

The ceiling ball is a good tactic for getting a little rest or driving your opponent back into deep-court. In the hands of some players, however, it becomes a suicide shot. If you try a ceiling shot from close in, center-court, say, you merely will give your foe an easy set-up shot that will blast a point out of your hide.

## CORRECTION

Don't be afraid of the ceiling shot. Just learn to use it from deep-court. It will drive your opponent back and give her nothing much to shoot at. When she makes a mistake, you can move in for a kill, a pass shot, or an otherwise sizzling corner return.

Practice ceiling shots by standing at mid-court and throwing the ball high to the back wall. Race back and get behind and to one side of the ball, forehand then backhand, and aim for those lights at the front end of the ceiling.

# MISTAKE

## Misjudging ceiling-ball distance

The ceiling shot looks simple yet has many possibilities for error. Hitting the ceiling ball too close to the side wall will allow it to bounce out into mid-court for an easy return (or worse) by your opponent.

It is easy to misjudge the distance from ball to racquet as you stroke the backhand ceiling shot. This sometimes makes for bad contact with the ball and a miss or inaccurate return.

It also is easy to let the ball come too close to your body so that you choke your swing just slightly—enough to make you miss the shot or set it up.

# CORRECTION

Use some of the time during a ceiling ball exchange to move your body sufficiently far from the ball to give you room for a complete swing.

This permits you to pay special attention to getting your body—especially shoulders and wrist—into the shot. It also will give you the control that rushing the shot or hitting the ball when it is a shade too close will never provide.

# MISTAKE

## Ceiling hypnosis

One of the worst problems in ceiling play is to become semihypnotized, or glaze-eyed, during an exchange of ceiling shots. You begin to watch the ball almost full time without also watching your opponent.

This gives him a great advantage. He knows where both you and the ball are. If you are in front of him, you only know where the ball is.

This works to your obvious disadvantage. He can easily bounce a shot behind you, out of your reach. He can pass you on the side or kill in one of the corners. Without noting where your opponent is, your shot will be chancy instead of directed toward a weakness in your foe.

# CORRECTION

A series of ceiling shots between two pros or other good players is one of the prettiest sights in racquetball. The game slows down to beautiful arcs and angles and affords a rest compared to the usual furious pace of a hard volley.

But the ceiling volley, aside from buying time, is a strategic weapon of great value to the would-be racquetballer. It can be a way of spotting an opening in your opponent's armor that you can immediately shoot into for a point.

To do this, however, you must at all times keep your eye on your opponent—and the ball. There's no better way to remember this than by keeping in mind the control advantage that this simple tactic offers you and the sad shape you'll be in if your opponent spots the "no-look" weakness in you!

# MISTAKE

## Overswinging on ceiling shots

Overswinging—hitting harder than is necessary—often plagues the ceiling shot volley. This shot is extremely tiring if used excessively, easily doing more harm to the player than the good rest that comes from slowing down the game.

# CORRECTION

The ceiling shot should be struck with just enough force to carry the shot to the back wall after a bounce. This is just enough force to keep your opponent back where it's relatively hard for him to kill, and it forces him to continue making defensive returns.

When working out alone, stand about three-quarters of the way back in the court and hit soft shots to the ceiling about three or four feet from where it meets the front wall. Determine the degree of force you need to get the ball back to the rear wall, and file the information for future use in your racquetball storehouse of knowledge.

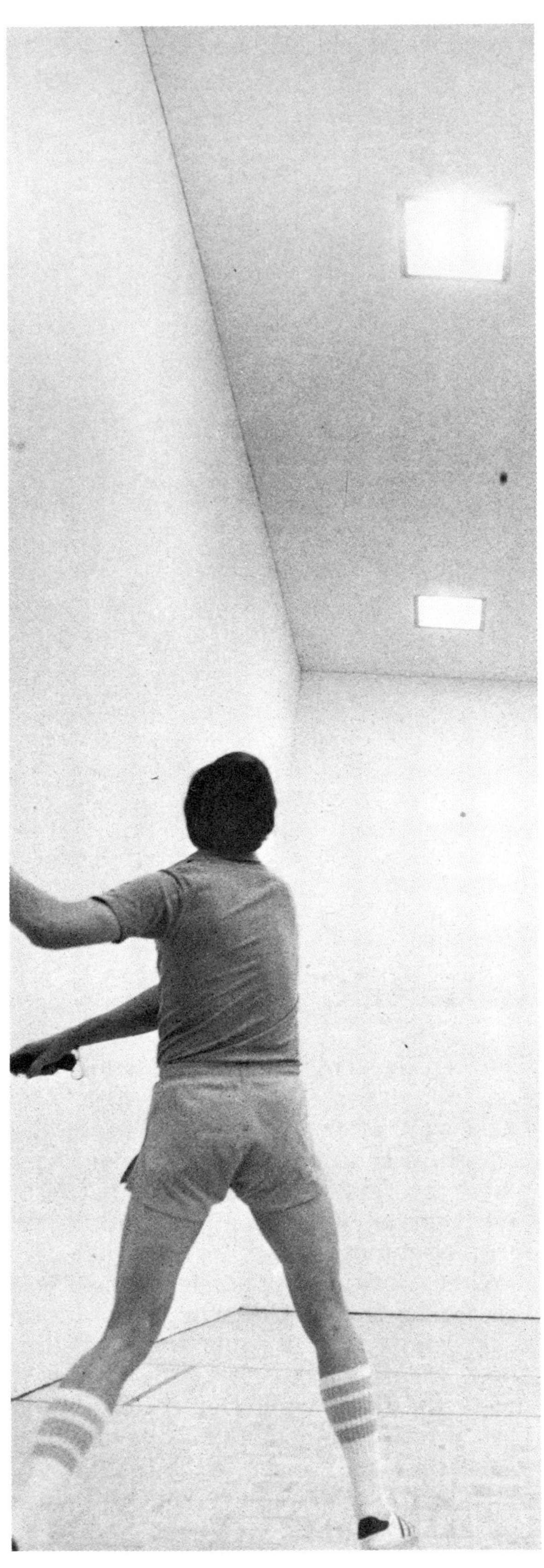

# MISTAKE

## Short ceiling shots

It is generally a strategic mistake to hit a "short" ceiling shot—one that hits short of the front four feet of the ceiling.

If considerably short, the shot won't even reach the front wall. If it barely makes it to the ceiling and front wall, it ends up in short-court, an easy set-up for a good opponent.

## CORRECTION

Most modern courts have a bank of light boxes in the ceiling about four feet out from the front wall. These make a good aiming point. Try to hit just ahead of them.

This should give you a shot with a high-bouncing arc that carries well into deep-court and forces your opponent to make a defensive shot instead of trying a kill.

# MISTAKE

## Using the backhand ceiling shot

The backhand ceiling shot of most players is generally a weaker, less accurate stroke than the forehand ceiling shot.

Don't be lazy and use the weaker backhand just because the ball seems headed to that side in deep-court.

Your chances of error on this return are considerably higher than when you use your forehand ceiling shot.

## CORRECTION

It may feel like a back-to-the-wall maneuver but it's only shoulder-to-the-wall. Unless it's a real "wallpaper ball" that clings to the side wall all the way back, chances are good that by pressing your shoulder to the wall you can hit an overhand ceiling shot with your forehand and make it count.

This will prevent weak or unpredictable backhand returns. It even may distress your opponent into trying to hit wallpaper balls down the side wall. He is bound to miss one of these, and the ball will carom off the wall into the clutches of your racquet for a good, low corner kill or pass.

# Chapter 8
# Hinders

# MISTAKE

## Charging

The Hinder—for hinderance—is a situation in which one player comes too close to another during play and hinders that player from having a clear shot at the ball.

Too many players, caught up in the heat of combat, keep charging the ball without regard to the position of their opponent—and cause injuries.

# CORRECTION

If there is the slightest doubt in your mind that body contact—or worse, racquet-on-body contact—may result from one of your swings, just (as the police say) FREEZE! STOP! AVOID!

Nothing is worth the risk of injury on the court. Many a friendship has gone down the drain on handball, squash, and racquetball courts because of the shouted word, "Hinder!"

In a nonrefereed match it is, or course, a matter that must be settled by the two players. In general, and according to the rules, a hinder is called only by the person who feels hindered.

The hinderer really doesn't have a say in the matter. But in practice, either player can and must call a hinder. Sometimes the hinderer is in a better position to see a dangerous situation coming up.

# MISTAKE

## Not calling hinder

In the heat of racquetball play, a player's determination to make a shot sometimes overrides his or her natural caution and results in one player running into another. The rules carefully make it mandatory for a player to get out of the way of the shooter to give him or her a clear shot.

When the shooter feels that he doesn't have a clear shot at the ball, he calls, "Hinder." Play stops and the point is started over again.

Not calling "Hinder" can result in injuries to both players and unnecessary friction.

# CORRECTION

Whenever it appears that making a shot will involve body contact, stop play and call, "Hinder."

In ordinary play without a referee, this gentleperson's normal call should suffice.

Later on, as you advance in racquetball, or after you've watched a tournament or two, you will see the wisdom of the "Hinder" call, and learn the "avoidable hinder," in which a player can lose the point for not getting out of the way of the shooter when it is possible to do so.

It's far better to call an excess of hinders than to risk a single injury.

Just stop cold, make your intentions clear with body language—such as the player with arms thrown up—and say, "Hinder."

It's one of the easiest and most important things to learn in racquetball.

# MISTAKE

## Not avoiding the avoidable hinder

Recently, racquetball borrowed a new rule from handball—the avoidable hinder rule. In brief, it is called when you could have gotten out of the way of your opponent and didn't. You can then lose a point at the referee's discretion.

The first time it was called in a pro match, against the immortal Charlie Brumfield by National Racquetball magazine editor and referee Chuck Leve, Brumfield was so shocked he could hardly go on, or acted that way!

# CORRECTION

If you can possibly get out of the way of the person hitting the ball, do so.

Experience is the only teacher in this situation.

The only rule you can follow to make avoiding avoidable hinders part of your game is to keep that head turning in the direction of the ball and your opponent so that their whereabouts are always known to you.

This makes it a simple matter to get out of their way.

When playing cut-throat (one player versus two) or doubles, avoiding other players becomes much more crucial than in singles, because the risk is twice as great with all those bodies on the court swinging those hard-edged racquets.

# Chapter 9

# Game strategy

# MISTAKE

## Freezing

There is a tendency on the part of many racquetball players to hit the ball and then freeze. Sometimes they feel that their shot was perfect, a kill or near kill, and there will be no return of the ball. Therefore, there's no reason to move is there? Wrong!

Freezing in position puts a player at a terrible disadvantage. Racquetball is a flowing, moving game. You must never assume a shot is "perfect" so you don't have to move into position for your next shot. It's usually a mistake to assume there will be no next shot.

# CORRECTION

One of the joys of racquetball to an aspiring player is the discovery of the center-court position. Center-court position is an invisible circle about six feet in diameter just past the short line in mid-court. It serves as a home base for pros, who range swiftly to all corners of the court. It's the place they come back to and from which they plan defenses and offenses. Mathematically it's pretty much equidistant from all the hot areas of the court, which makes it the fine strategic headquarters that it is.

After making a shot, it's a good idea to scoot down to that center-court position and run your game from there, leaving when you must but returning quickly. Keep moving. That's what makes you alert enough to play the game well.

# MISTAKE

## Abusing center-court position

It's not enough to have an understanding of the center-court position as a headquarters area on the racquetball court.

You mustn't take that position blindly and expect all your problems to be solved. In the excitement of doing something right a new player often forgets one of the basics. In the case of center-court position the forgotten basic is: keep your eye on the ball and on your opponent at all possible times.

You've made it to center-court position but have forgotten to take quick, head-turning glances at your opponent. Wham! He shoots the ball down one side or the other, and you can't get there in time because, by not looking, you haven't been able to get a good jump on the shot.

## CORRECTION

Keep that head swiveling and hang loose. Don't get set and plant your feet. Be ready to move at all times, and, of course, keep watching the ball and your opponent.

You can pick up a whole step's lead and more by watching him set up and shoot for the front wall. You can start for one or the other corner and be there in time to make an effective return.

# MISTAKE

## Badly positioned kill shot

You are near mid-court with your opponent behind you. A ball comes to your forehand. You have the correct impulse to kill the ball—but you try to kill it right up the middle. The ball doesn't quite go in as a perfect kill and emerges in beautiful position for your opponent's deadly return shot. Your kill try was too close to your opponent.

## CORRECTION

You must always be aware of where your opponent is and where she can get to from where she is. You also must allow for the possibility that your kill attempt will not be perfect.

This should convince you to try to kill away from your opponent, in this case to the right front corner of the court. Even if your kill isn't perfect, its speed and carom from side wall to front wall will work for you. Most of all, the fact that you hit away from your opponent, not toward her, will raise the odds in your favor.

So try for perfection—the perfect kill or pass—but also have an instant Plan B in mind—and use it!

Great chess players think eight or nine moves ahead. Of course they have more time than racquetball players, but you should be able to think *one* shot ahead. The idea is the same: planning pays off.

# MISTAKE

## Compounding errors

Beginning players often bring to racquetball a preposterous looking series of built-in mistakes. These can be errors in stance, in swinging, in grip, or in almost any other department of the game.

If the more costly of these errors (in terms of points and proficiency) aren't corrected early in the learning process, they harden and become part of the player's "game."

# CORRECTION

In the absence of a good teacher, the aspiring player should watch other reasonably good players and read the available instructional material—usually available at the desk of every court club or Y.

The point is to develop a smooth, effortless swing that "feels" good. A mirror will help you examine your basic form. Does it look smooth? Are you standing sideways to a real or imagined wall both for forehand and backhand?

In actual play, if you feel a leg pull up into the air wildly each time you hit the ball or feel your elbow bend awkwardly with the terrible consistency of any bad habit, hen, even without an instructor, you know what you have to practice.

Take the court by yourself. Use yourself as your own opponent. Slow down your body's movements as you approach the ball, and try to iron out the kinks you *feel*. If you can't feel what's wrong, have the club pro or other good player or friend watch you and tell you what he or she thinks is keeping your game from being a series of smooth maneuvers.

# Chapter 10
# Doubles

# MISTAKE

## Doubles troubles

Doubles is a difficult game for the beginner because it adds an element of sharing responsibility. "Yours!" and "Mine!" are the only two words that should be spoken during a volley, says U. S. R. A. President Bob Kendler.

But who gets which shot?

The possibilities for disaster in the shot that comes right up the middle between two partners are obvious.

# CORRECTION

Generally, the player on the forehand side should take the shot that comes down the middle between two partners. Forehands are generally better developed than backhands, but this may vary from team to team. The better stroke should have preeminence.

The Kendler practice of "Yours!" and "Mine!" should be followed.

# MISTAKE

## Doubles coverage

As in any combat situation, the placement of the troops is vital for victory in racquetball. In doubles, both team members often follow the ball up and back on the court, as if they were both going to swing at the same shot every time.

## CORRECTION

One partner should play up and one farther back. In this way much more of the court can be covered than if both partners move up and back simultaneously with the movement of the ball.

The relative speed and shot-making abilities of partners soon become apparent. Which partner plays up and which plays back can be decided—or the roles can be alternated.

# Index